THE CURIOUS CONNECTORS

*Powerful Questions to Ask
When Networking*

FROM THE EXPERTS
AT MBX

Edited by Lil Barcaski

Published by: GWN Publishing
www.GWNPublishing.com

Cover Design: Kristina Conatser Captured by KC Designs

ISBN: 978-1-959608-87-5

TABLE OF CONTENTS

FOREWORD: THE POWER OF TRUE CONNECTIONS

by Forbes Riley

Welcome, dear reader, to a journey that transcends the mundane and delves into the realm of meaningful human connections. As you flip through the pages of this book, you're about to embark on an adventure that will unravel the secrets behind forging genuine bonds that stand the test of time.

But, before we dive headfirst into the depths of this exploration and meet some amazing co-authors, allow me to share a little secret with you—one that has been the cornerstone of my own journey: the philosophy of reaching out to people when you don't need them, so they are there when you do.

Now, I know what you're thinking: It sounds counterintuitive, right? Why would anyone bother to connect with others if they don't immediately need something from them? Well, my friend, that's precisely where the magic lies.

You see, true connections aren't built on transactional exchanges or fleeting encounters. And as I am politely called, The Queen of Pitch, because of my success in sales in home shopping and infomercials, many people misconceive that I am always "pitching." Perhaps I am, see for me, pitching is not "selling" - I define the perfect pitch as a conversation that excites, engages and enrolls people. Sometimes it's to enroll them into their own greatness, passions and purpose... that's why I'm so committed to getting people just like you to understand the power of the pitch. See, if you truly nurture your relationships through genuine interest, shared experiences, and mutual respect, they will last forever. And what better way to cultivate these connections than by reaching out simply to connect, to learn, to share, and to uplift one another?

I learned this invaluable lesson early on in my journey, and it's served me well ever since. Whether it was striking up conversations with strangers at networking events, reaching out to industry leaders for advice, or simply lending an ear to a friend in need, I've always approached every interaction with an open heart and a genuine desire to connect.

And let me tell you, the results have been nothing short of miraculous. From forging lifelong friendships to securing game-changing partnerships, the power of true connections has opened doors I never even knew existed.

Now, you may be wondering what sets this book apart from the myriad others on the subject of networking and relationship-building. Well, my friends, let me introduce you to the mastermind behind this collaboration—none other than my dear friend and "masterful connector," Blaney Teal.

Blaney is not just a connector; she's a force of nature—a whirlwind of energy, passion, and boundless enthusiasm. Her ability to bring people together, to foster meaningful connections, and to create opportunities where others see obstacles is nothing short of awe-inspiring. Now you mix that with her newest venture of creating an exotic retreat venue in sunny Mexico and we can all network in style!

I was inspired to offer my two cents to help introduce Blaney's book and it's precisely this spirit of collaboration and community that infuses every page. From the heartfelt anecdotes shared by fellow authors to the practical strategies and insights gleaned from years of collective experience, each chapter is a testament to the power of true connections in both professional and personal realms.

So, dear reader, as you embark on this journey of discovery, I urge you to approach it with an open mind and an open heart. Be willing to step outside your comfort zone, to embrace the unknown, and to connect with others in ways you never thought possible.

Because when you do, you'll not only unlock the secrets to making true connections but also discover a world of endless possibilities waiting to be explored.

Here's to the power of connection, the magic of collaboration, and the beauty of forging bonds that last a lifetime.

With boundless enthusiasm and a sprinkle of stardust,

Forbes Riley

✉ ForbesRiley@gmail.com
🌐 www.ForbesRiley.com
🌐 www.ForbesRileysTrainings.com

"Queen of the Perfect Pitch"

TV Host, Dr. Forbes Riley is a pioneer and industry leader in the field of infomercials and Home Shopping TV, with product sales of over $2.5 billion. A true Renaissance Woman, best-selling author, and high-performance results coach, she started her stellar career on TV and movies as an actress. Today she teaches and trains entrepreneurs to level up THEIR communication skills for themselves and the world, taking people from zero to hero in their personal and professional relationships. As a keynote motivational speaker, she has been compared to Tony Robbins for her bold, dynamic style that instantly transforms audiences.

She has shared stages with Les Brown, Deepak Chopra, Mel Robbins, Jack Canfield, Grant Cardone, and Shark Tank's Daymond John. Forbes is a True Global Thought Leader and Brand on a mission to ignite Hope and Prosperity.

Join Forbes LIVE every Sunday for her Pitch Like Pro Masterclass https://bit.ly/ForbesMasterclass

Or check out her latest Speaker Certification Course: https://mbx.events/speakercert

MESSAGE FROM THE FOUNDER

by Blaney Teal – MBX Founder

Welcome to the "MBX Collaboration Book." Within these pages, you'll discover a wealth of insights shared by our esteemed MBX Members. As you journey through this book, we invite you to uncover valuable golden nuggets that can transform your approach to networking and collaboration.

In 2017, I founded Making Business Connections (MBX) with a vision to revolutionize networking. Tired of the traditional "sales pitch" atmosphere and the superficial interactions resembling dating events, I set out to create a space where genuine connections and meaningful collaborations thrive. This book is a testament to that vision, showcasing the collective wisdom and experiences of our vibrant MBX community.

In the realm of business networking, the mere act of exchanging business cards has become somewhat of a cliché. While having a stack of cards can be useful, true networking transcends this transactional approach. It's about building meaningful connections that go beyond surface-level interactions.

At its core, effective networking is about establishing relationships based on trust, mutual benefit, and genuine interest. It's about listening intently to others' stories, understanding their needs, and offering value in return. This mindset shifts the focus from self-promotion to collaboration and support within a professional community.

Networking events and virtual platforms provide opportunities to meet new people, but the real magic happens when these encounters evolve into lasting connections. Following up with a personalized email or scheduling a one to one meeting to delve deeper into shared interests can significantly enhance the networking experience.

Moreover, active participation in industry-related discussions, volunteering for projects, and offering assistance when needed are pillars of successful networking. It's about being present, engaged, and proactive in nurturing relationships that can lead to fruitful collaborations and business opportunities.

TAKE A MOMENT TO CONSIDER THIS: Who in your network could benefit from connecting with a new contact you've made? And what valuable insights can you share that might make a positive impact on their business?

In this book, we are going to introduce you to a fresh approach of connecting with people that you meet through in-person and virtual networking.

Before you go any further, follow these steps to ensure that you get the most out of this book and the experts found within.

STEP 1: Business Connector App-FREE for the first 60 days: https://mbx.events/bookapp or scan the QR Code

When it asks you if you are part of a group/network, select **YES** and **MBX** (this will get you special perks).

STEP 2: Click on the green button and get your basic account FREE for 60 days. This is special pricing for all readers!

STEP 3: Set up YOUR KnoCard by adding your profile picture, contact information, and business information. This may include external links, a social post, and media files that introduce you and your business to our experts plus other members and Knocard users.

STEP 4: Download the KnoCard app from the Apple or Google Play Store to enable mobile features. (Do not do this until you have gotten your account in Step 1 or you'll miss out on MBX perks.)

STEP 5: As you go through each of the chapters, identify the members who resonate with you and connect with them directly through your KnoCard. You will be able to get access to their contact info as well as more info about them on their Knocard. Simply search by name and select the contact to follow or message. You can even send a referral if you'd like! Be sure to connect with ME!

And lastly, I invite you to attend a MBX Networking Event (in-person or virtually) You can check out our calendar of upcoming events by scanning or going to the link below. We'd love to see you inside our community!

https://mbx.events/calendar

Here's to successful networking!

Blaney Teal

Blaney Teal

Founder of Making Business Connections (MBX)

https://mbxevents.com

Meet the
MBX EXPERTS

SUPERSTARS

SUPERSTAR

Colleen Strube

COMPANY: Connect Develop Succeed, LLC

TITLE: Follow-Up Fortune Finder

MBX AREA CONNECTOR: Frederick County, MD

🎁 **FREE TICKET TO FALL IN LOVE WITH FOLLOW-UP:**
*The Secret to Building Lasting Relationships
and Success in Business Workshop (Value $97):*
https://www.connectdevelopsucceed.com/bookgift

BIOGRAPHY

I'm described as many things: connector, trainer, coach, entrepreneur, wife, mother, and friend.

I empower professionals and entrepreneurs from all over the world to gain more leads, set more appointments, and obtain more clients while building authentic relationships.

When I worked in the corporate IT field, I loved training and supporting my clients because I could make a difference for them with my great problem solving and communication skills. Even though I loved what I was doing, I didn't have control of my time. I felt like I was missing out. I wanted to spend more time with my three boys and husband and still provide some financial support to the family.

That's when I decided to start my own business. Nervously, I went to my 1st networking event on 9/11/2001 (yes that 911). I'm not sure why but I felt compelled to return the following week which started my journey to becoming a Master Connector. After struggling for a while, I discovered I didn't have the resources or know enough people to be successful. I felt overwhelmed and stuck.

As I attended networking events and met amazing people, I realized there were three areas to master:

1. Finding the right place to network

2. Knowing what to say & do at events

3. Following-up and building relationships

While I was creating the solutions to these problems, I gained knowledge and expertise.

> Earned a Master in Business Administration

> Founder/Creator of Connect Develop Succeed, LLC

> Certified BeeKonnected Expert

> Certified MinkLife Networking Influence Booster Trainer

> Certified B.A.N.K. IOS Coach

> Excel at Relationship Development

> Master Connector at 5000+ networking events in 25 years

Because of that, people call me the Networking Queen and I know everyone. Well, not everyone but I'm working on it because I'm passionate about helping others to realize that connections are key.

That's why I created my signature Connect Develop Succeed framework and my Fall in Love with Follow-Up Program. These programs help my clients to connect consistently and develop relationships with lead generation and nurturing.

So, are you struggling with this right now? Where will your next connection come from? Let's schedule a call so I can learn more about you and your business. I'm happy to share some secrets and insights on how to grow your network.

IF YOU'D LIKE TO CONNECT WITH COLLEEN, SCAN HER KNO-CARD NOW.

Where is the most offbeat or weirdest place you have made a networking connection?

In my 25-plus years of networking, I've made connections in some pretty random spots – think waiting rooms, airports, gyms, even concerts. But one of the weirdest places? Hands down, it's gotta be the bleachers at my kids' baseball games.

Back when I was just starting out in my network marketing gig, I used to bring those monthly product flyers with me to the games. You know, the ones I had to slap address labels on, stamp, and tape shut? Yeah, those ones. So, there I'd be, sitting in the stands, multitasking like a pro – cheering on Daniel, Spencer, and Jason while prepping envelopes.

But here's the kicker: those baseball games turned out to be goldmines for networking. Every time I busted out my flyers, some other mom would inevitably ask me what the heck I was doing. And just like that, I had my opening to talk about my products and business.

I even made sure to carry a product with me, just to pique people's interest. It was crazy how those games became my unofficial networking events. Sure, I miss watching my boys play ball, but I sure as heck don't miss sending out those flyers.

Nowadays, networking's a whole different ball game – pun intended. No more paper flyers; it's all about shooting off a quick text with a link to a video or website. But you know what? Despite all the fancy tech, nothing beats those good ol' days on the bleachers, chatting up other baseball moms and making connections without even trying.

What out of the norm ways can you suggest to new networkers to find connections?

Start connecting while you're simply living your life. One of the most valuable pieces of networking advice I've ever received is to embrace opportunities to meet new connections in everyday settings.

Whether you're hitting the gym, attending a school event, or jetting off on a trip, keep your eyes and ears open to the possibilities around you. Strike up conversations with fellow gym-goers between sets, chat with other parents at your child's school function, or engage fellow travelers in conversation during your commute.

The key is to be open-minded and genuinely interested in the people you meet. Approach each interaction as an opportunity to learn something new or make a meaningful connection. You never know where a chance meeting might lead or what doors it could open in your professional or personal life.

So, don't limit your networking efforts to formal events or professional settings. Instead, seize every opportunity to connect while you're out and about living your life. Who knows? Your next big connection could be just a conversation away.

What is/are your favorite social media platforms for networking and what tips can you offer to make connections on social media?

Let's dive into the world of social media networking – it's like a virtual goldmine, the ultimate playground for connecting with potential clients, partners, and investors from all over the world. With so many platforms available – Facebook, LinkedIn, Instagram, Alignable, and the list goes on – it's easy to feel overwhelmed. Here are some tips to help you navigate the social media maze and make meaningful connections.

First things first, find your tribe. Where are your ideal clients and strategic partners hanging out? Which platform(s) resonate with them? Keep in mind, each platform has its own vibe and audience, so choose the ones that align best with your personality and business goals. Whether you're all about the professional vibes of LinkedIn or the visual storytelling of Instagram, there's a platform out there that will help you leverage your time on social media to reach your business goals.

Now, when it comes to making connections on social media platforms, remember this mantra: social first, business second. Building relationships is key, so take the time to engage with others, share valuable content, and show genuine interest in what they have to say. Trust me, the business connections will naturally follow. It's all about striking the right balance between showcasing your expertise and building meaningful connections. You don't want to land yourself in social media jail.

In addition to Social Media platforms, there are now Social Business Platforms like BeeKonnected and KnoCard. These platforms were designed specifically for businesses and the primary focus is on fostering connections and collaborations that drive business growth. While relationship-building remains paramount, the overarching goal is to leverage these connections to advance your business objectives, whether it's securing new clients, forming strategic partnerships, or accessing funding opportunities. They offer a unique opportunity to connect with like-minded professionals and expand your network in meaningful ways along with the opportunity to monetize your following through affiliate and your own programs.

So, whether you're navigating established social media platforms or exploring innovative social business platforms, the underlying principle remains the same: prioritize relationship-building, stay true to yourself, and provide value with your content. By leveraging social media effectively, you can unlock a world of opportunities to expand your network and propel your business forward.

What tips can you offer a new networker that will help them shine when networking?

Here are just some of my tips to help you be productive and make a good impression while networking.

ONLINE NETWORKING:

Mind Your Virtual Manners: Avoid eating during virtual meetings or events. While it may have been acceptable at in-person lunches, it can be distracting and unprofessional on camera.

Stay Focused: Resist the urge to walk around or engage in distracting activities while on camera. Maintain focus and attention on the conversation at hand to foster meaningful connections.

Set the Scene: Pay attention to your surroundings and background when participating in virtual meetings. Choose a clutter-free and professional backdrop to convey competence and professionalism.

IN-PERSON NETWORKING:

Early Bird Advantage: Arrive early to in-person events to maximize networking opportunities. Use this time to familiarize yourself with the venue and engage with key individuals.

Make Introductions: Take the initiative to introduce yourself to the event organizer, speakers, and influencers present. These individuals can be valuable connections and may open doors to future opportunities and collaborations.

Volunteer Your Support: Offer to assist the organizer or speaker in any capacity they may need. Not only does volunteering showcase your willingness to contribute, but it also provides an opportunity to stand out and leave a lasting impression.

By following these tips, you can navigate networking events with confidence and professionalism, leaving a positive impression on those you meet. If you're eager to dive deeper and explore a personalized approach tailored to your unique needs, I'd love to connect with you. Let's chat and uncover how we can collaborate to achieve your goals. Reach out to me, and let's start this exciting journey together.

What are three friendly questions to ask during a one-on-one meeting with a new connection to start a conversation naturally?

I love to ask people "What do you do for fun?" This question will offer you some insights into their interests and hobbies, which will help you understand them on a personal level. When they reciprocate and ask what I do for fun, I share my enthusiasm for networking and meeting new people. By learning more about them, I'm able to determine how I can support them and their business. When they ask you, what will you answer?

I also like to ask, "What problems do you solve and who benefits from your solutions?" Don't be surprised if this question catches them off guard. In my networking experience, a lot of networkers when asked what they do answer with a title like I'm a business coach, realtor, insurance rep, etc. By asking them what problems they solve will prompt them to articulate their business offerings in terms of solving problems for their clients. It's an opportunity for them to clarify their expertise and ideal clientele. Understanding their niche enables you to better support and refer them within your network, strengthening your relationship.

When doing a 1-1 meeting, I ask "What's currently working great in your business?" By asking this question, you invite your connection to share their achievements and successes. Everyone loves to celebrate their wins, and this question allows them to do just that. As they share, actively listen for opportunities where you can offer support or assistance. Additionally, inquire about areas that are not working as well or where they'd like to improve.

By incorporating these questions into your one-on-one meetings and networking, you'll not only break the ice in a non-salesy or intrusive manner but also deepen your understanding of your connection and their business, paving the way for meaningful collaboration and support.

Tips for Crafting Memorable Networking Intros?

When it's your turn to shine with a 30 or 60-second 'commercial' at a networking event, it's crucial to make every second count. I found several strategies that have helped myself and my clients and maybe they can help you too.

Respect the Time Limit: Keep your pitch concise and focused. Respect the time constraints to ensure you capture and maintain the audience's attention throughout.

Start Strong: Begin by grabbing the audience's attention right from the start. You can achieve this by posing a thought-provoking question or sharing a compelling statistic related to your industry or niche.

Introduce Yourself Clearly: State your name clearly and confidently. Then, clearly describe who you help and how you provide value to them. Even if you offer multiple services, focus on highlighting one key offering to avoid overwhelming your audience.

Engage with a Call to Action: Conclude by reinforcing your name and delivering a clear, strong call to action. Encourage your listeners to take a specific next step, whether it's scheduling a consultation, visiting your website, or connecting with you on social media.

By adhering to these guidelines and crafting a compelling and clear pitch, you'll ensure that your 'commercial' leaves a lasting impression on your audience, making you memorable and increasing the likelihood of meaningful connections and opportunities.

The expression goes, The Fortune is in the Follow-up! What ways have you found most effective when to keep in touch with people you meet at networking events? Do you have any follow-up no no's that should be avoided?

Yes, The Fortune is in the Follow-Up and I realized if you want to succeed you need to Fall in Love with Follow-up. As I mentioned before, I've been networking for decades. However, for years the mere mention of the word 'follow-up' sent a wave of dread coursing through me.

Despite accumulating stacks of business cards, countless "zoom" chats, and a vast network of social media connections, I found myself falling short of my desired results. I was wasting opportunities because I wasn't following up. I lacked a structured follow-up system.

So, I experimented with various follow-up methods, I initially attempted reaching out immediately post-event, only to find myself drained of energy or hurriedly rushing to the next engagement. Sound familiar? I then tried scheduling dedicated follow-up time but struggled to maintain consistency or found myself sidetracked by other obligations or distractions.

The turning point came when I acknowledged the flaw in my approach. While many view follow-up as a mere business transaction, I shifted my perspective. I began to see it as the essential next step in nurturing authentic relationships – a mindset shift that transformed my approach entirely. Now, I was reaching out to see how I could serve my connections and they appreciated the follow-up.

The last challenge was to find the time to follow-up. Remember, if you don't follow-up, you are wasting your time and money networking. Ultimately, I discovered the transformative power of community. Bringing together supportive professionals and leveraging valuable resources, I created an environment where everyone involved could thrive. Thereby, finding our fortune in the Follow-Up while having fun doing it.

Anything else you'd like to share around being a Curious Connector not covered above.

To wrap things up, here are a couple of key reminders. First off, building relationships is at the heart of it all – remember, connections are key. When it comes to follow-up and networking, having the right mindset, a solid system, and an action plan are crucial.

You've probably heard the saying that people do business with those they know, like, trust. I add the word remember. It's important to add that last part – being remembered. Even if someone knows, likes, and trusts you, if they can't recall you when they need your services, it doesn't really matter. So, make sure you leave a lasting impression and stay top-of-mind with your network.

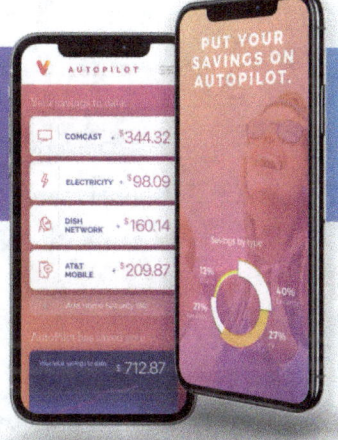

SUPERSTAR

Stacey Butler

COMPANY: Stacey Butler Co.

TITLE: Business Choreographer and Systems Strategist

MBX AREA CONNECTOR: Houston, Texas

🎁 **FREE GIFT:** *access to my Simplify and Apply BizTech Mastery Hub*
https://l.bttr.to/M63M8 *Use Promo Code CCBook100*

BIOGRAPHY

Hello, I'm Stacey Butler, the Business Choreographer and architect of business efficiency. I'm not just a strategist; I revolutionize the way wellness professionals and coaches navigate the complexities of their business backend. With the artistry of a choreographer and the precision of a systems strategist, I empower you to streamline your operations and amplify your success. Imagine your business as a dance floor where I guide you through each step, ensuring every move is a strategic leap towards efficiency and impact.

I am all about creating easy tech solutions and straightforward strategies that fit just right for you. I am here to help your business not just succeed, but also to make your life more balanced, so you can do your best for your clients. I'm here to help you sort out the complicated stuff and set up systems that make everything easier.

As your strategic partner, I fine-tune your processes to simplify your tech experience and empower you to focus on what you do best—cultivating your business with confidence and a clear plan of action.

Are you ready to reclaim your time and focus on what truly matters in your business? Let's have a virtual coffee chat. Together, we will craft a tailored strategy that aligns with your ambitions and refines your systems for an outstanding and efficient performance.

IF YOU'D LIKE TO CONNECT WITH STACEY, SCAN HER KNOCARD NOW.

Where is the most offbeat or weirdest place you have made a networking connection?

The most offbeat place I've connected was during a long-haul flight. It's fascinating how a casual conversation with the person seated next to you can evolve into a business opportunity or a valuable addition to your network.

What out of the norm ways can you suggest to new networkers to find connections?

I personally encourage new networkers to embrace creativity when forging new connections. Imagine yourself hosting or participating in virtual events, like webinars or interactive workshops, to not only share your expertise but also to connect with an audience that's just right for your message. Volunteering for causes that mirror your business's core values can lead to discovering new relationships with individuals who are just as passionate as you are. I believe in the idea of 'value first'—it's a powerful draw for meaningful connections. By adopting these fresh and innovative networking strategies, you have the opportunity to broaden your professional network in ways that old-school methods just can't match.

What is/are your favorite social media platforms for networking and what tips can you offer to make connections on social media?

Personally, I find LinkedIn and Instagram to be incredibly powerful for making connections, but I also have a soft spot for the road less traveled, exploring platforms like Alignable, BeeKonnected, and Knocard. To truly shine on these platforms, ensure your profile is meticulously crafted with a professional photo and a bio that succinctly yet powerfully encapsulates your expertise—think of it as your own digital calling card. When you share content that educates, inspires, or entertains, you're not just posting; you're positioning yourself as a beacon for thought leadership, attracting those who resonate with your vision. Authenticity in engagement is my mantra; dive into the dialogue with meaningful comments, share content that adds value, and be responsive to foster genuine connections. And remember, the personal touch of a direct message after an initial public exchange can be the key to unlocking deeper, more fruitful opportunities.

What tips can you offer a new networker that will help them shine when networking...- Online?- In person?

Envision each interaction as a chance to not merely meet someone new, but to truly engage with them on a deeper, more personal level. I believe that the art of attentive listening is paramount. Picture yourself sharing a coffee with a close friend—you wouldn't be preoccupied with your upcoming schedule or distracted by your phone. You'd be fully present, offering them the gift of your undivided attention. This is the level of engagement you should bring to your networking encounters. Hear their narratives, empathize with their obstacles, and celebrate their victories as if they were your own. Pose inquiries that demonstrate your genuine interest and involvement in their discourse. When you listen with the purpose of comprehending rather than merely replying, you weave a thread of authenticity into the connection. This method not only enriches the conversation for both individuals but also establishes a foundation for a professional relationship that has the potential to thrive.

What are three friendly questions to ask during a one-on-one meeting with a new connection to start a conversation naturally?

1. "I'm always curious to hear about people's journeys. How did you get started in your current role, and what do you love most about what you do?"

2. "Are you working on any passion projects?"

3. "What do you do for fun?"

Tips for Crafting Memorable Networking Intros?

I've learned that the initial moments of a networking interaction can set the stage for a meaningful connection. I like to begin with something that not only captures attention but also reveals a bit of who I am—perhaps an intriguing fact, a question that reflects my curiosity, or a bold statement that hints at my passion for innovation. I then share what I do in a way that's easy to grasp, highlighting how my unique approach can make a real difference, without getting bogged down in industry speak.

But what really brings my introduction to life is a personal story or a testimonial from someone I've worked with. This isn't just about what I do; it's about the impact it has on real people and businesses. I choose words that are full of life and movement, aiming to stir emotions and create a memorable image in the listener's mind. Finally, I extend an invitation to continue our conversation, whether that's a one-on-one meeting or a suggestion to explore my website for a more comprehensive understanding of my services. It's all about making that human-to-human connection.

The expression goes, The Fortune is in the Follow-up! What ways have you found most effective when to keep in touch with people you meet at networking events? Do you have any follow-up no no's that should be avoided?

I've come to appreciate that the real magic of networking lies in the follow-up. It's not just about collecting business cards; it's about building bridges. When I connect with someone at an event, I make it a point to send a follow-up that's as unique as our interaction. I'll often reference a specific discussion we had or a mutual interest, which shows I'm genuinely interested in the connection we've made.

I also set personal reminders to reach out at intervals, not just when I need something, but to share resources or opportunities that could benefit them. It's about adding value to their professional lives, which in turn strengthens our relationship.

As for what I avoid, I never send those cookie-cutter emails that feel like they've been blasted to a thousand inboxes. They're impersonal and miss the mark. And I'm careful not to overstep by bombarding someone with messages. Patience and respect are my watchwords here; I let the relationship evolve at a comfortable pace for both parties.

Anything else you'd like to share around being a Curious Connector not covered above.

I approach networking with the philosophy that it's about cultivating authentic relationships, not merely amassing contacts. When I meet someone new, I think about how I can contribute to their success. Can I offer insights, make a helpful introduction, or provide a resource that aligns with their goals? By focusing on being of service, I find that my network expands naturally. This approach ensures that each connection is rooted in mutual benefit and respect, which is the cornerstone of any lasting professional relationship.

Nina Boucher

COMPANY: EssentiallyForMe

TITLE: Chief Appreciation Advisor

🎁 **FREE GIFT:** *Send a free card to anyone in the world*
https://www.SendOutCards.com/u/essentiallyforme/send

BIOGRAPHY

Imagine being top of mind, memorable and referrable. That's what we help you achieve: feel and stay connected with the Power of a Card, for both personal and business growth.

Now picture yourself feeling healthy, lean and living green. We show you how with the Power of a Drop.

As a relationship developer, Nina strives to help others improve their relationships with self and others because she believes "There's more happiness in giving than...in receiving". This bilingual funpreneur is what folks consider to be their personal appreciation advisor, and their creative collaborator for their business.

IF YOU'D LIKE TO CONNECT WITH NINA, SCAN HER KNOCARD NOW.

Where is the most offbeat or weirdest place you have made a networking connection?

On vacation and in planes may not be so offbeat for some but it could be as it was for me especially when starting out. I hadn't quite been in the mindset that if you're a networker, there's no real vacation from that because it becomes a lifestyle and that's a good thing. So when on vacation, I had to transition out of "I don't want to talk about work here" mode because when work is fun, why wouldn't you want to share it now?

What out of the norm ways can you suggest to new networkers to find connections?

When living in a city, there's times when buses, trains, etc. may face delays. In such occasions, using a lot of tact, seeing if a conversation can be started, will not only pass the time but possibly present itself as an opportunity to make connections. If living in rural places, get out of your comfort zone to go to local events that may not even interest you with the intent to grow and learn. You'd be surprised by the people you meet and could connect with!

What is/are your favorite social media platforms for networking and what tips can you offer to make connections on social media?

Honestly this is an area I hope to improve on and I know I'm not alone. So dear reader, rest assured that we're all a work in progress! But I'm looking forward to connecting with folks over offbeat platforms that may not be considered mainstream yet such as BeeKonnected and Clapper. I know that regardless of the platform, consistency is the absolute key! I myself am hoping to implement my new goals in this regard which is 4 steps: first, engage; then post; check-in routinely in between and use a timer! Lol, it's too easy to get time sucked into a rabbit hole!

What tips can you offer a new networker that will help them shine when networking?

Have the goal to learn and contribute regardless if online or in person. Never expect a sale! It might sound counterproductive but it should come as a side benefit of being genuinely interested in helping the other person in some way. When you have that mindset of "how can I be of service?", your mood, your energy, your words are felt differently and is more welcoming

What are some friendly questions to ask during a one-on-one meeting with a new connection to start a conversation naturally?

In order to break the ice, I like to start with a compliment or an observation that we can further discuss, especially if it was an article or blog they wrote, something they said or did, etc. I also have found that asking for their brief help is a great way to welcome their expertise and to share their tips. Sometimes I will also ask about their pets. For most people, their pets are family and a great neutral member to talk about. Plus you can learn a lot from a person within the context of that conversation.

Tips for Crafting Memorable Networking Intros?

Tailor your pitch or commercial to your audience. Sometimes we get into the bad habit of trying to cram EVERYTHING we do. But less is more and build from that. I've had to work on that and it evolves over time with lots of practice. Also, start with the benefits in mind. Paint that picture briefly for your audience and leave them wanting more. Leaving a bit of a cliffhanger can initiate questions later.

The expression goes, The Fortune is in the Follow-up! What ways have you found most effective when to keep in touch with people you meet at networking events? Do you have any follow-up no no's that should be avoided?

My favorite follow up tool is sending cards with a print on demand system I use. As soon as the meeting is over, if at all possible, a card goes out to remind them of our connection. There's just something different about receiving that tangible touch! Set a reminder date to continue checking in too.

Also, take notes! You will meet lots of people. You will go to lots of events. How will you remember any of these people if you didn't take 5 minutes to take notes? I don't know about you but I sure know my memory won't retain it all as I'd like. So use your phone's voice feature to input keywords into the person's contact info. Your future self will thank you when you remember that great tip they gave you, or remember your shared admiration of an author/book, or remember what shared interest and passions you have. Folks, these are your relationship building blocks right here! Develop this habit and you'll notice how much easier it is for you to refer others to them and/or vice versa.

My big no-no is to sell them right away. Oh, it's so distasteful! Build the relationship first, before any sale.

Anything else you'd like to share around being a Curious Connector not covered above.

Dear reader and networker, just have fun! You're not alone in this journey and we all keep growing, getting better and better. With drops of love and paper smiles, I hope to see you online or in person sometime.

Laura Lee Kenny

COMPANY: Blue Diamond Club LLC

TITLE: Money Mindset Mentor

BIOGRAPHY

Born at the end of the Baby Boomer era in rural New Brunswick, Canada. We had a very large family of 12 children, and no silver spoon. In fact, I started working for other people when I was 12 years old.

Certified Financial Planner for over 20 years, where I guided clients to reach their financial goals and prepare for retirement. I teach financial literacy and I'll tell you, that we all need to know about this. Let me show you how to up-level your income bracket. There are so many ways to earn money and save on taxation. I'm on a crusade to learn more ways myself, so I can teach others to do the same thing. Affiliate marketing is a great way to start.

When we start taking care of our money at a young age, it is so easy to guide people to become millionaires. Even the average wage earner can easily become wealthy if they have the desire to change their mindset.

Additionally trained with dozens of mentors over the years, such as Jim Rohn, Tony Robbins, Bob Proctor, Christy Whitman, Forbes Riley, Conrad Brem, and many Mindvalley courses. Certified with Marissa Peer, as an RTT in hypnosis in Dec 2016. Graduated Year 1, Donna Eden Energy method in Jan 2019. Also, a Certified Destiny Coach with Peggy McColl in 2021. Founding member of More Value Now in Dec 2022.

Three-time International Best-selling co-author with Thrive and Prosper, Empowered Women in Business, and Becoming an Unstoppable Woman in Finance in 2022.

CEO of Blue Diamond Club L.L.C.

IF YOU'D LIKE TO CONNECT WITH LAURA LEE, SCAN HER KNO-CARD NOW.

Where is the most offbeat or weirdest place you have made a networking connection?

A PRACTICAL GUIDE TO NETWORKING SUCCESS IN THE MODERN DAY.

Welcome, my fellow wallflowers and social butterflies, to the whimsical world of networking! In this chapter, we'll embark on a delightful journey filled with laughter and invaluable networking tips. So, grab your favorite beverage, settle into your comfiest chair, and let's spread our wings and soar to new heights in the world of networking!

UNCONVENTIONAL NETWORKING: FROM QR CODES TO CHANCE ENCOUNTERS

Networking isn't confined to stuffy conference rooms, stiff handshakes, or formal events – sometimes, the most memorable connections happen in the most unexpected places. Let's navigate the networking maze with laughter, genuine curiosity, and perhaps a touch of the unexpected. Picture this: you're standing in line at the grocery store, mindlessly scrolling through your phone, which is glued to your hands these days, when suddenly, you strike up a conversation with the person behind you about the merits of organic vs. non-organic produce. Before you know it, you've exchanged contact information and promised to grab coffee sometime. Who knew networking could be so fruitful (pun intended)? I've learned that opportunities to network are everywhere – you must be open to them.

What out of the norm ways can you suggest to new networkers to find connections?

OUT-OF-THE-NORM WAYS TO FIND CONNECTIONS

Now let's talk about some unique strategies to help new networkers spread their wings and expand their circle of connections:

1. **Volunteer Work:** Engaging in volunteer activities not only allows you to give back to your community but also exposes you to a diverse range of people from different backgrounds and industries. Whether you're serving meals at a homeless shelter or helping out at a local animal rescue, volunteering can lead to meaningful connections with like-minded individuals who share your values.

2. **Ask for Interviews:** Informational Interviews with leaders in an industry, as they are well-connected to other top leaders. A wealth of knowledge and experience can be gained by listening to top leaders. Utilize Alumni Networks by connecting with fellow graduates.

3. **Professional Development Courses:** It is essential that we continually improve our education and uplevel our skills. Enroll in some online virtual courses where you can connect in breakout rooms.

4. **Collaborative Projects outside your immediate network:** Attending Niche Events related to your hobbies or personal interests, in person or online, puts you in front of new eyeballs. Be open to new BFF's, Business Friends Forever.

5. **Dog Park Networking:** For our furry friends and their human companions, dog parks offer a unique opportunity to network in a relaxed and informal setting. While your furry sidekick frolics with their canine pals, strike up conversa-

tions with fellow dog owners and bond over your shared love of four-legged friends.

6. **Fitness Class Connections:** Whether it's a yoga class, spin session, or dance workshop, fitness classes provide a fun and active environment for networking. Break the ice by complimenting someone's downward dog or striking up a conversation about your favorite workout playlist. Who knows, you might just find your next workout buddy and business partner rolled into one!

7. **Community Garden Gatherings:** If you have a green thumb and a passion for gardening, why not join a local community garden? Not only will you get to indulge your love of gardening, but you'll also have the opportunity to connect with fellow garden enthusiasts and swap tips, tricks, and maybe even homegrown produce.

8. **Virtual Cooking Classes:** In the age of Zoom and virtual gatherings, why not sign up for a virtual cooking class? Not only will you learn new culinary skills, but you'll also have the chance to connect with fellow foodies worldwide. Bond over your shared love of gourmet cuisine and swap recipes and cooking hacks.

What tips can you offer a new networker that will help them shine when networking?

SOCIAL MEDIA SAVVY: MAKING CONNECTIONS IN THE DIGITAL AGE

Ah, social media – the modern-day water cooler where professionals gather to connect, share insights, and build relationships. But with so many platforms to choose from, where should you focus your networking efforts? Fear not, my friends, for I have some tips to help you navigate the digital landscape with ease and I'll share some pros and cons about my experiences. Many people choose more than one platform:

1. LinkedIn: Ah, the holy grail of professional networking. LinkedIn is a go-to platform for connecting with industry peers, sharing insights, and showcasing your expertise. To make the most of LinkedIn, be sure to complete your profile, engage with relevant content, and join industry groups to expand your network

2. X: Despite its character limit, X is a powerful networking tool for engaging in real-time conversations with thought leaders and industry influencers. Use hashtags to join industry-specific conversations, retweet valuable content, and interact with fellow professionals to expand your network. I find it very challenging to engage with strangers. It is very straight to the point and here's my sales page. Very little connecting. It is like people are selling water in a desert.

3. Instagram: While Instagram may be known for its visual content, it's also a great platform for networking, especially for creative professionals. Showcase your work, share behind-the-scenes glimpses of your life, and engage with followers and fellow creatives to build meaningful connections. It also seems to be a much younger crowd and more social than business.

4. Facebook Groups: Facebook groups are a treasure trove of networking opportunities, with countless groups dedicated to every industry, niche, and interest imaginable. Join relevant groups, participate in discussions, and offer value to establish yourself as a valuable community member. I find it difficult to get noticed by serious buyers, especially because the algorithms are always changing, and they only allow about 5% of your friends and followers to see your posts and content. And they like to put people in jail. Some

entrepreneurs have even had their accounts shut down for voicing their health concerns about COVID-19 shots or political opinions.

5. Clubhouse: A newer option, Clubhouse is an audio-based social networking app where users can join virtual rooms to participate in live discussions and panels. Join industry-related rooms, share your expertise, and connect with like-minded professionals in real-time conversations. Because it is audio only, I miss the virtual aspect of looking into someone's eyes and reading the body language.

6. BeeKonnected: The Coolest Kid on the Block. It is a combination of many of these platforms and everybody can see 100% of your post! Now that's amazing. BeeKonnected is a fantastic platform for making meaningful connections in the business world. BeeKonnected offers a unique blend of social networking and professional development, making it an ideal space for entrepreneurs, professionals, and business owners to connect and collaborate. You can live stream to other platforms without having to have Streamyard. You will have your own video and audio program, that eliminates the expense of Zoom and Streamyard, at no extra charge. It has clickable links built into the platform, so whether live or on replays, your links are clickable, which will take customers to your checkout page to purchase your inventory. You can have Public or Private Groups. Host your own podcast or TV show for an unbelievable introductory price. And you can host your courses to sell to the entire database. Plus, it is Monetized, so you will get paid when you upgrade to affiliate status. Your referrals generate affiliate commissions when they upgrade to a paid account on 2 tiers! It also has an AI Konnection generator that matches you up to your ideal connections based on the information you give the program and chat in groups or private messages. It is exciting to be on the ground floor of the coolest tech-

nology company out there. So easy to get noticed and grow your following. This is my favorite playground, in this social media business arena. Where you won't get put in jail or suspended unless you do something illegal or immoral. There are no pesky bots or scammers allowed on the platform. I've found my home. Come check it out and grab your FREE account. https://TheKennys.beekonnected.com/

What tips can you offer a new networker that will help them shine when networking?

SHINE BRIGHT LIKE A SOCIAL STAR: THE ART OF BEING UNFORGETTABLE!

Networking effectively, whether online or in person, requires a combination of strategy, communication skills, and genuine engagement. Here are some tips to help new networkers shine in both scenarios:

ONLINE NETWORKING:

1. **Optimize Your Profile:** Ensure your online profiles on platforms or professional networking sites are complete and professional. Use a clear, professional photo and craft a compelling bio that highlights your skills, experiences, and expertise.

2. **Engage Actively:** Participate in online discussions, forums, and groups related to your industry or interests. Share valuable insights, ask questions, and contribute to conversations to establish yourself as a knowledgeable and engaged member of the community. Also, connect and get noticed by industry peers.

3. **Personalize Connection Requests:** When reaching out to connect with someone online, personalize your connection request. Mention a mutual interest or connection, and explain why you'd like to connect and find common ground. Personalized requests are more likely to be accepted by establishing rapport and building meaningful connections.

4. **Offer Value:** Focus on providing value to your online connections. Share relevant articles, resources, or insights that you think would be beneficial to them. By offering value, you'll position yourself as a helpful and valuable connection worth maintaining. Silence is not golden here.

5. **Follow Up Promptly:** After making new connections online, follow up promptly with a personalized message. Thank them for connecting, express your interest in getting to know them better, and suggest a virtual coffee chat or informational interview to further the relationship.

IN-PERSON NETWORKING:

1. **Be Approachable Aura:** First Impressions Matter. Smile and make eye contact while maintaining an open body language to appear approachable and friendly. Approach others with confidence and initiate conversations by introducing yourself and finding common ground to build upon.

2. **Prepare Elevator Pitch:** Have a concise and compelling elevator pitch ready to introduce yourself effectively in person. Highlight your skills, expertise, and what you're looking to achieve professionally clearly, and engagingly.

3. **Active Listening:** When engaging in face-to-face conversations, practice active listening. Show genuine interest in the person you're speaking with, ask thoughtful questions, and listen attentively to their responses. This demonstrates

respect and fosters meaningful connections. Remember, we have 2 ears and 1 mouth for a reason.

4. **Exchange Contact Information:** Don't forget to exchange contact information with new connections you meet in person. Whether it's exchanging business cards, QR codes or connecting on any social media platform, ensure you have a way to stay in touch and continue building the relationship beyond the initial encounter.

5. **Follow Up with Gratitude:** After networking events or meetings, follow up with a thank-you email or note to express gratitude for the opportunity to connect. Reference something specific from your conversation to personalize the message and leave a positive impression.

By following these tips, new networkers can confidently navigate online and in-person networking opportunities and effectively build meaningful connections in their professional circles.

What are three friendly questions to ask during a one-on-one meeting with a new connection to start a conversation naturally?

Initiating a one-on-one meeting with a new connection can be a delicate balance between building rapport and gathering useful information. Here are 3 icebreaker questions that are non-salesy and respectful of boundaries:

1. **"What initially drew you to [their profession or industry]?":** This question allows your new connection to share their professional journey and passions without feeling pressured to discuss specific business transactions or sales pitches.

2. **"What is your escape from the 9-5?"**: This question shifts the conversation to personal interests, allowing for a more relaxed and authentic exchange. It demonstrates a genuine interest in getting to know the person beyond their professional identity.

3. **"Have you come across any interesting books, articles, or podcasts lately?"**: This question opens the door for discussing shared interests or learning opportunities. It's a subtle way to gather insights into their interests and potentially discover common ground.

Tips for Crafting Memorable Networking Intros?

Crafting an effective 30 or 60-second "commercial" or elevator pitch is crucial for making a lasting impression at networking events. Here are some strategies to present yourself memorably and engagingly:

1. **Start with a Hook:** Begin your commercial with a compelling hook that grabs attention and piques curiosity. This could be a thought-provoking question, a bold statement, or a relatable anecdote that sets you apart from the crowd. Especially lose the Ego, "I am", and swap out for "As a" instead.

2. **Highlight Your Unique Value Proposition:** Clearly articulate what sets you apart and makes you unique in your industry or field. Focus on the specific skills, experiences, or accomplishments that demonstrate your value to potential connections or employers.

3. **Keep it Concise and Clear:** Be mindful of the time constraint and keep your pitch concise and to the point. Avoid jargon or technical language that might confuse your audience, and focus on communicating your message clearly and effectively.

4. **Use Vivid Language and Examples:** Incorporate vivid language and concrete examples to illustrate your points and make your pitch more memorable. Paint a picture of who you are, what you do, and how you can help others in a way that resonates with your audience.

5. **Inject Passion and Enthusiasm:** Infuse your pitch with energy, enthusiasm, and passion for what you do. Show genuine excitement about your work and convey your enthusiasm in a way that is contagious and memorable.

6. **End with a Call to Action:** Conclude your pitch with a clear call to action that prompts your audience to take the next step. Whether it's scheduling a follow-up meeting, connecting on social media, or exchanging contact information, make it easy for people to engage with you further.

7. **Practice, Practice, Practice:** Practice delivering your pitch until it flows naturally and confidently. Rehearse in front of a mirror, with a trusted friend, or record yourself to fine-tune your delivery and ensure you come across as polished and professional.

8. **Personalize for the Audience:** Tailor your pitch to the specific audience or context of the networking event. Highlight aspects of your background or expertise that are most relevant to the people you're speaking with, and make connections to their interests or needs whenever possible.

By incorporating these strategies into your 30 or 60-second commercial, you can effectively present yourself in a way that captivates attention, makes a memorable impression, and sets the stage for further networking opportunities.

The expression goes, The Fortune is in the Follow-up! What ways have you found most effective when to keep in touch with people you meet at networking events? Do you have any follow-up no no's that should be avoided?

We firmly believe in the power of follow-up to solidify connections and unlock opportunities. Here are some effective ways to keep in touch with people you meet at networking events:

1. **Send a Personalized Email:** After the event, send a personalized email to each person you met, thanking them for the conversation and expressing your interest in staying connected. Reference something specific you discussed to demonstrate that you value the interaction.

2. **Connect on Their Favorite Platform:** Send connection requests to your new contacts, including a personalized message reminding them of where you met and expressing your interest in networking further. BeeKonnected & LinkedIn are valuable platforms for maintaining professional relationships and staying updated on each other's activities.

3. **Schedule a Follow-Up Meeting:** If you had a particularly meaningful conversation with someone at the networking event, suggest scheduling a follow-up meeting or coffee chat to continue the discussion. This shows your genuine interest in building a deeper connection beyond the initial encounter.

4. **Engage on Social Media:** Follow your new contacts on other social media platforms where appropriate, such as Twitter or Instagram, and engage with their posts by liking, commenting, or sharing relevant content. Social media provides additional touchpoints for staying connected and building rapport.

5. **Attend Mutual Events or Workshops:** Keep an eye out for future events or workshops that your new contacts may be

attending and make an effort to attend those as well. Meeting in person again reinforces your connection and provides an opportunity for further networking.

While follow-up is crucial, certain approaches should be avoided to ensure your interactions remain professional and respectful:

1. **Overly Persistent Communication:** While it's important to follow up, bombarding your new contacts with excessive emails, messages, or phone calls can come across as intrusive and off-putting. Respect their time and boundaries by allowing for space between communications.

2. **Being Too Transactional:** Avoid approaching follow-up interactions with a purely transactional mindset focused solely on what you can gain from the relationship. Instead, strive to build genuine connections based on mutual respect and shared interests.

3. **Ignoring Boundaries or Cues:** Pay attention to any cues or signals that indicate your new contacts may not be interested in further communication. Respect their boundaries and avoid pushing for continued engagement if they seem unresponsive or disinterested.

4. **Sending Generic Messages:** Generic follow-up messages that lack personalization or relevance can easily be overlooked or disregarded. Take the time to craft thoughtful, personalized communications that demonstrate your genuine interest in building a meaningful connection.

By employing these effective follow-up strategies and avoiding common pitfalls, you can nurture your networking relationships and harness the full potential of your professional connections. Remember, the fortune truly is in the follow-up when it's done with authenticity, respect, and professionalism.

Anything else you'd like to share around being a Curious Connector not covered above.

We can't emphasize enough the importance of adopting the mindset of a "Curious Connector" in your networking endeavors. Here are some additional insights and tips to further enhance your networking approach:

1. **Embrace Curiosity:** Approach networking with genuine curiosity and a thirst for learning. Ask thoughtful questions, actively listen to others, and seek to understand their perspectives, experiences, and challenges. Curiosity fuels meaningful conversations and fosters deeper connections.

2. **Be Open to Serendipity:** Stay open to serendipitous encounters and unexpected opportunities that may arise in your networking journey. Keep an open mind, be flexible, and embrace the potential for chance meetings or connections that could lead to exciting possibilities.

3. **Facilitate Connections:** Act as a facilitator of connections within your network by actively connecting people who could benefit from knowing each other. Whether it's making introductions, sharing resources, or recommending colleagues for opportunities, facilitating connections demonstrates your value as a connector and strengthens your relationships.

4. **Stay Current and Informed:** Stay informed about industry trends, developments, and emerging technologies to enrich your conversations and provide value to your network. Share relevant articles, insights, and resources with your connections to demonstrate your expertise and keep them engaged.

5. **Seek Diverse Perspectives:** Seek out connections from diverse backgrounds, industries, and perspectives to broaden your horizons and enrich your network. Embracing diver-

sity fosters creativity, innovation, and a more inclusive network that reflects the complexity of the modern business landscape.

6. **Follow Up with Curiosity:** When following up with new connections, approach the conversation with curiosity and a genuine interest in learning more about them and their work. Ask insightful questions, seek to understand their goals and challenges, and look for opportunities to support and collaborate.

7. **Invest in Relationships:** Building meaningful relationships takes time and effort. Invest in nurturing your network by staying in touch, showing appreciation, and offering support when needed. Remember, networking is not just about transactions—it's about building lasting connections based on trust and mutual respect.

Dr. Rhonda Farrell

COMPANY: Global Innovation Strategies

TITLE: Success Strategist

🎁 **FREE GIFT:** *The Secret to Scaling Your Business to 7-Figures:*
https://tinyurl.com/scaleyourbiz7fig

BIOGRAPHY

Dr. Rhonda Farrell is a distinguished success strategist and coach, acclaimed for steering individuals and organizations toward achieving 7-Figure success milestones. Her dedication to unlocking the vast potential within people has led to transformative results, characterized by her inventive methods, insightful guidance, and steadfast commitment.

Holding a rich academic and business background, Dr. Farrell has carved her niche as a success strategist, collaborating with leaders and entrepreneurs from diverse sectors, including commercial enterprises, non-profits, and governmental bodies. Her journey is fueled by a relentless curiosity and a genuine desire to aid others in navigating the complexities of success, establishing her as a pioneer in the domain of holistic transformation.

Dr. Farrell offers transformative coaching, workshops, and speaking engagements, designed to unleash the untapped talent and creativity within her clients. Her methodology integrates advanced neuroscience, proven business strategies, and age-old wisdom, aiming for not just financial achievement but also comprehensive personal and professional development.

Her ability to foster a mindset geared towards success and provoke meaningful action has earned her recognition from a wide spectrum of professionals, from emerging entrepreneurs to veteran leaders, all of whom attribute a part of their success to her guidance. Beyond her professional accolades, Dr. Farrell is renowned for her philanthropic efforts, striving to uplift marginalized communities across various sectors.

As a respected thought leader, Dr. Farrell's insights reach a broad audience through her publications, enriching readers with the knowledge to unlock deeper aspects of their potential. Her active engagement in non-profit initiatives and entrepreneurial accelerators further solidifies her reputation as a reliable expert in achieving success.

Driven by an unwavering pursuit of excellence, Dr. Rhonda Farrell is continuously setting new standards of success, impacting lives, and fostering significant transformations. Her legacy, characterized by visionary strategy and coaching, stands as a testament to her extraordinary commitment and the profound influence she has on individuals and the broader community.

IF YOU'D LIKE TO CONNECT WITH DR. RHONDA SCAN HER KNOCARD NOW.

Where is the most offbeat or weirdest place you have made a networking connection?

Exercising in the pool not only rejuvenated my body but also unexpectedly fostered very valuable networking connections. As I swam laps, I struck up conversations with fellow hot tub gatherers and swimmers who happen to share my industry. Our discussions on healthy lifestyles seamlessly transitioned into professional matters, leading to a productive exchange of ideas and contact information. This chance encounter transformed into flourishing and ongoing networking connections, speaking opportunities, and illustrates the serendipitous power of combining physical wellness with meaningful professional relationships.

The pool can be a fantastic place to connect with people for consulting and coaching purposes due to several unique factors:

1. **Relaxed Atmosphere:** The pool provides a relaxed and non-formal setting, which can help people let their guard down and engage in more open and authentic conversations. This comfortable environment fosters genuine connections.

2. **Shared Activity:** Engaging in a physical activity like swimming creates an immediate common ground. Sharing an

activity can break the ice and make it easier to start a conversation, especially for those who might be more reserved in traditional networking settings.

3. **Natural Segues:** Conversations can naturally flow from discussing the activity (swimming) to broader topics, including personal goals, challenges, and aspirations. This progression creates a smooth transition to coaching and consulting discussions.

4. **Mind-Body Connection:** Swimming promotes mental and physical well-being, and conversations in such an environment can lead to discussions about holistic success strategies, self-care, and achieving a balanced lifestyle.

5. **Time for Reflection:** Swimming allows for periods of solo activity and reflection, creating opportunities for individuals to think about their goals and potential areas where coaching or consulting could be beneficial.

6. **Less Formal Pressure:** Unlike traditional business settings, the pool is a place where people often feel less pressure to adhere to formalities. This can lead to more authentic and unguarded interactions, making it easier to establish trust.

7. **Shared Experiences:** Overcoming challenges in the pool (such as learning to swim or improving technique) can parallel the challenges people face in their personal or professional lives. These shared experiences provide a basis for meaningful conversations.

8. **Positive Associations:** Pools are often associated with relaxation, leisure, and enjoyment. This positive atmosphere can enhance the overall mood and receptivity to discussions about personal growth and success.

9. **Memorable Connections:** Unconventional networking settings like the pool can leave a lasting impression, making the

encounter more memorable and enhancing the likelihood of ongoing interactions.

10. **Adaptability:** Poolside conversations can be tailored to different personality types and communication styles. Some may prefer casual chats, while others might engage in deeper discussions – your approach can adapt to each individual.

Utilizing the pool as a networking and connecting environment for consulting and coaching purposes can help create unique, genuine, and memorable interactions that lay the foundation for meaningful and transformative relationships.

What out of the norm ways can you suggest to new networkers to find connections?

For new leaders and entrepreneurs, creating valuable connections requires innovative strategies beyond traditional networking events.

Here are some out-of-the-norm ways to build your network and foster meaningful professional relationships:

1. HOST A VIRTUAL ROUNDTABLE OR WEBINAR

Organize an online roundtable discussion or webinar on a pressing issue or trend in your industry. Invite thought leaders, entrepreneurs, and professionals to contribute, fostering a collaborative environment where connections naturally form.

2. ENGAGE IN CROSS-INDUSTRY INNOVATION LABS

Participate in or create innovation labs that bring together leaders from different sectors to tackle global challenges. These labs are hotbeds for creative thinking and can lead to powerful collaborations and partnerships.

3. LEVERAGE EXECUTIVE RETREATS

Attend or organize executive retreats that focus on personal development, leadership, and industry insights. These settings offer a unique blend of relaxation and professional growth, conducive to building deeper connections.

4. INITIATE A MASTERMIND GROUP

Create or join a mastermind group with leaders and entrepreneurs from various industries. These groups offer mutual support, advice, and accountability, building strong professional relationships based on shared growth and challenges.

5. CONTRIBUTE TO INDUSTRY THINK TANKS

Engage with think tanks related to your field. Participating in research, discussions, and policy development can introduce you to a network of influential professionals committed to driving change.

6. ORGANIZE A COMMUNITY IMPACT PROJECT

Lead a project that addresses a local community issue, inviting other professionals to join your cause. Projects that have a social impact can forge connections based on shared values and community service.

7. PARTICIPATE IN OR HOST HACKATHONS

Even if you're not in the tech industry, hackathons can be an excellent way to meet innovative thinkers and problem solvers. Hosting a hackathon to solve industry-specific problems can attract a diverse set of skilled individuals.

8. CURATE AN EXCLUSIVE INDUSTRY NEWSLETTER

Create a newsletter that provides insightful analysis on trends affecting your industry. An insightful newsletter can establish you as a thought leader and become a platform for engaging with other leaders and professionals.

9. ATTEND OR SPEAK AT TEDX EVENTS

TEDx events bring together people from various fields to share ideas worth spreading. Attending or speaking at these events can elevate your profile and connect you with other forward-thinking individuals.

10. UTILIZE MENTORSHIP PLATFORMS

Offer mentorship through platforms that connect experienced professionals with emerging leaders and entrepreneurs. This can be a fulfilling way to meet ambitious individuals and give back to your industry.

11. ENGAGE WITH PROFESSIONAL CLUBS AND SOCIETIES

Join or engage with exclusive clubs and societies that cater to professionals and leaders. These organizations often host events, dinners, and talks that facilitate high-level networking.

12. EXPLORE COLLABORATIVE WORKSPACES

Beyond typical co-working spaces, look for collaborative workspaces that focus on bringing together entrepreneurs, artists, and professionals from diverse fields. These spaces often host community events and workshops that can be fertile ground for networking.

13. PARTICIPATE IN ADVENTURE NETWORKING

Join or organize networking events based on adventure sports or activities (e.g., hiking, sailing, or rock climbing). These shared experiences can build camaraderie and open the door to professional discussions in an unconventional setting.

14. DIGITAL NOMAD MEETUPS

If you're able to work remotely, join digital nomad communities and attend their meetups around the globe. These communities are full of entrepreneurial individuals who value flexibility, innovation, and the exchange of ideas.

By stepping outside the traditional networking playbook, leaders and entrepreneurs can discover rich opportunities for connection and collaboration that align with their unique paths and visions. The key is to remain authentic and open to the potential of every interaction.

What tips can you offer a new networker that will help them shine when networking?

For new professional leaders and entrepreneurial networkers, making a lasting impression in both online and in-person settings is crucial for building meaningful connections and expanding their network.

Here are tailored tips to help them shine:

ONLINE NETWORKING

1. **Optimize Your Digital Presence:** Ensure your LinkedIn profile and other social media platforms reflect your current professional interests, achievements, and the value you can

provide. A professional photo, compelling summary, and detailed experience section can set you apart.

2. Contribute Valuable Content: Share insights, articles, and posts that contribute to conversations in your field. This not only showcases your expertise but also sparks engagement and attracts like-minded professionals.

3. Engage Actively: Comment on posts, congratulate connections on their achievements, and participate in relevant groups and forums. Your active participation demonstrates your interest in your field and your willingness to engage in the community.

4. Host Virtual Events: Webinars, virtual meetups, or roundtable discussions on topics of your expertise can establish you as a thought leader and create a platform for engaging with others.

5. Leverage Direct Messaging: Reach out to potential mentors, peers, or industry leaders with personalized messages. Highlight common interests or how their work has inspired you to make the connection feel genuine.

IN-PERSON NETWORKING

1. Prepare Your Elevator Pitch: Have a clear and concise way to introduce yourself and what you do. Tailoring your pitch to the context and audience can make it more effective.

2. Listen More Than You Speak: Show genuine interest in others by asking questions and actively listening to their responses. This approach builds rapport and makes your interactions memorable.

3. Follow Up: After meeting someone, send a personalized follow-up message or email. Mention something specific from

your conversation to reinforce the connection and propose a next step, such as a coffee meeting or a call.

4. **Attend Diverse Events:** Beyond industry-specific events, attend meetups, workshops, and seminars on a variety of topics. Diverse environments can lead to unexpected and valuable connections.

5. **Volunteer:** Offer your skills or time to organize events or take on leadership roles in professional groups. This visibility can attract others who are interested in your skills and leadership style.

6. **Dress Appropriately:** First impressions matter. Dressing appropriately for the event and industry can help you feel confident and leave a positive impression.

7. **Carry Business Cards:** Even in a digital age, having a business card can facilitate the exchange of contact information and serve as a tangible reminder of your encounter.

8. **Be Authentic:** Authenticity is compelling. Share your passions, challenges, and experiences genuinely. People are drawn to authentic leaders and are more likely to remember and want to connect with them.

9. **Practice Empathy:** Show empathy and understanding in your conversations. Recognizing and acknowledging the challenges or successes of others can build deeper, more meaningful connections.

10. **Stay Open to Serendipity:** Be open to conversations and connections, even if they don't seem immediately relevant to your goals. The most serendipitous encounters can lead to valuable opportunities and friendships.

Networking is a skill that improves with practice and intention. Whether online or in person, the key is to approach each interaction with curiosity, openness, and a genuine desire to build a relationship, not just a contact list. By providing value and showing interest in others, you'll not only shine in networking situations but also lay the foundation for a strong and supportive professional network.

What are three friendly questions to ask during a one-on-one meeting with a new connection to start a conversation naturally?

Navigating one-on-one meetings with new connections requires tact, especially for professional leaders and entrepreneurs looking to make a positive and lasting impression.

Here are three questions designed to break the ice in a way that's engaging and respectful, without veering into overly personal or uncomfortable territory:

1. "WHAT INSPIRED YOU TO PURSUE A CAREER IN [THEIR INDUSTRY]?"

This question opens the floor for a narrative response, inviting the person to share their personal journey and motivations. It's a great way to learn about their passions and the driving force behind their career choices, providing insights into their values and personality.

2. "CAN YOU SHARE A CHALLENGE YOU'VE OVERCOME IN YOUR PROFESSIONAL JOURNEY AND WHAT YOU LEARNED FROM IT?"

Asking about challenges and the lessons learned offers a deeper look into their professional resilience and problem-solving skills. It fosters a conversation grounded in shared experiences of overcoming obstacles, potentially revealing areas where you might offer support or advice, and vice versa.

3. "LOOKING AHEAD, WHAT'S ONE EXCITING DEVELOP-MENT OR GOAL YOU'RE WORKING TOWARDS IN YOUR CAREER OR BUSINESS?"

This forward-looking question encourages them to share their aspirations and any upcoming projects or goals. It not only provides insight into their ambitions and what matters to them but also opens opportunities for you to explore potential collaborations, offer resources, or share relevant connections.

Each of these questions is designed to initiate meaningful dialogue that goes beyond superficial small talk. They encourage sharing of professional experiences and personal insights in a manner that's engaging, respectful, and mutually enriching. By focusing on aspirations, challenges, and motivations, you're more likely to foster a connection that is based on mutual respect and potential collaboration, rather than coming across as salesy or intrusive.

The expression goes, The Fortune is in the Follow-up! What ways have you found most effective when to keep in touch with people you meet at networking events? Do you have any follow-up no no's that should be avoided?

Turning networking encounters into enduring professional relationships hinges on inventive and thoughtful follow-up strategies. Here's how to elevate your approach and steer clear of common missteps, ensuring your follow-up not only resonates but also cements connections made at leadership or entrepreneurship events.

INNOVATIVE FOLLOW-UP APPROACHES

1. **Prompt, Yet Thoughtful Contact:** Initiate contact within 24 hours, but with a twist. Alongside your message, share a digital token of your meeting—a photo from the event or an infographic that ties into your conversation.

2. **Craft a Memorable Message:** Ditch the template. Compose a message that resonates on a personal level, perhaps by quoting something they said or linking to a song or a piece of art that your conversation reminded you of. It's about creating a connection that sticks.

3. **Be a Resource:** Position yourself as a hub of information and resources. Share an insightful article, podcast episode, or a tool that addresses a challenge they mentioned. Even better, create and share a mini-curated newsletter tailored to their interests.

4. **Innovate on LinkedIn:** When connecting on LinkedIn, do more than just send a request. Publish a post highlighting your key takeaways from the event and tag them with a note of thanks for the insights they shared. It's public recognition and connection in one go.

5. **Propose a Unique Next Step:** Instead of the usual coffee meet-up, suggest a more memorable activity related to your shared interests. Think a virtual escape room, a private webinar with an industry leader, or a collaborative project.

6. **Master the Art of Timing:** Establish a rhythm in your follow-up that keeps you on their radar without overcrowding it. Use tools like CRM software to remind you when it's time to touch base, ensuring you're remembered for the right reasons.

FOLLOW-UP MISTAKES TO SIDESTEP WITH CREATIVITY

1. **Avoid the Sales Pitch Trap:** Leap over the direct pitch. Instead, invite them to a brainstorming session on a mutual interest or challenge, offering a platform for collaboration before transaction.

2. **Personalize Beyond the Norm:** Elevate beyond the standard personalization. Share something you learned from them in a creative format, like a mini-podcast episode or a short video, making the follow-up uniquely memorable.

3. **Balance Your Enthusiasm:** Craft a follow-up cadence that intrigues rather than inundates. Consider integrating interactive content, like quizzes or polls related to your industry, to engage them without overwhelming.

4. **Honor Your Promises Creatively:** If you've promised to connect them with someone or send information, do it with flair. For instance, arrange a three-way virtual coffee or send the information within an interactive PDF or a creative slideshow.

5. **Navigate Social Media With Care:** When connecting on social media, do so with a novel approach. Share a piece of content they've created with your network, with a note about what you found valuable, inviting them to connect on a deeper level.

6. **Adapt to Their Communication Style:** If they have a preferred communication style, mirror it with innovation. If they prefer brief updates, consider a micro-podcast or a series of short, engaging videos to share updates or ideas.

By infusing your follow-up strategy with creativity and personalization, you transform standard networking follow-ups into memorable interactions that pave the way for strong, lasting professional relationships. This innovative approach not only distinguishes you from the crowd but also builds a foundation of mutual respect and collaboration.

Anything else you'd like to share around being a Curious Connector not covered above.

Being a "Curious Connector" is a powerful approach for professional leaders and entrepreneurs aiming to build meaningful relationships and foster a vibrant network.

This mindset revolves around genuine curiosity, empathy, and the intent to connect people not just for personal gain, but to create mutual value.

Here are some additional insights and strategies to enhance your role as a Curious Connector:

CULTIVATE GENUINE CURIOSITY

> **Embrace a Learner's Mindset:** Approach every interaction with the belief that there's something valuable to learn. This openness can lead to unexpected insights and deeper connections.

> **Ask Open-Ended Questions:** Encourage others to share their stories, challenges, and aspirations by asking questions that prompt reflection and detailed responses. This not only shows your interest but can also reveal areas where you can offer support or collaboration.

FOSTER EMPATHETIC CONNECTIONS

> **Practice Active Listening:** Truly listen to understand, not just to respond. This helps in recognizing the emotions and values behind words, building a stronger rapport.

> **Share Vulnerably:** Be willing to share your own experiences, including failures and lessons learned. Vulnerability can foster trust and encourage others to open up.

CONNECT WITH INTENT

> **Map the Ecosystem:** Keep an internal map of the skills, needs, and interests of the people in your network. This makes it easier to connect individuals who can benefit from each other's expertise or experience.

> **Facilitate Introductions:** When making introductions, provide context on why you think the individuals should connect and how they might help each other. A warm and thoughtful introduction can set the stage for a fruitful relationship.

LEVERAGE TECHNOLOGY WISELY

> **Use Digital Tools to Enhance Personal Connections:** While digital platforms can help manage your network, remember that the goal is to enhance personal connections. Use technology to remember personal details, follow up effectively, and share relevant opportunities or information.

> **Curate Content Thoughtfully:** Share or create content that adds value to your network. This could be industry insights, personal reflections on leadership, or resources for personal and professional development.

EMBRACE DIVERSITY

> **Seek Diverse Perspectives:** Actively seek to connect with individuals from different backgrounds, industries, and ex-

perience levels. Diverse perspectives can inspire innovation and provide a richer understanding of complex issues.

> **Host Inclusive Conversations:** Organize forums, roundtables, or virtual meetups that encourage diverse participation. Creating a space where different voices are heard can lead to richer discussions and stronger connections.

CONTINUOUS GROWTH

> **Invest in Your Development:** Stay curious about your own growth as a leader and connector. Engage in continuous learning through courses, reading, and seeking feedback from your network.

> **Reflect Regularly:** Take time to reflect on your experiences as a connector. Consider what's working well, what challenges you've faced, and how you can improve in facilitating meaningful connections.

Being a Curious Connector is not just about expanding your network; it's about deepening the connections within it and creating a community where support, knowledge, and opportunities flow freely. By fostering a culture of curiosity, empathy, and intentional connection, you can build a network that not only supports your professional growth but also contributes to the growth of others.

Meet the

MBX EXPERTS

PROS

PRO

Lowell Sheets

COMPANY: Sheets and Associates

TITLE: Owner

MBX AREA CONNECTOR: Harford County, MD

BIOGRAPHY

Lowell Sheets is an Entrepreneur, Business Coach, Author, Speaker, and Internet Marketing Strategist.

He is a 'Marketing Magician' online with Sheets and Associates, a Baltimore marketing agency, helping businesses to get found online with 5-star reviews and convert visitors into clients for life.

He is also a professional magician as TheMagicBartender.com and TheMagicMC.com, providing laughter and amazement at corporate, private, charity, wedding, and trade show events.

IF YOU'D LIKE TO CONNECT WITH LOWELL, SCAN HIS KNO-CARD NOW.

Where is the most offbeat or weirdest place you have made a networking connection?

I've made networking connections while performing magic illusions at corporate and private events.

What out of the norm ways can you suggest to new networkers to find connections?

LinkedIn searches are often effective to find meaningful and profitable connections. Answering questions that prospects pose, can also set you up as an expert in the field.

What is/are your favorite social media platforms for networking and what tips can you offer to make connections on social media?:

My favorite social media platform for creating connections and strengthening relationships is Facebook. One high-level tip is to search through contact's birthdays and be the first to wish someone a happy birthday, even 3 to 5 days before. It will be so unusual and so unexpected; you will be remembered and your relationships can blossom from there.

What tips can you offer a new networker that will help them shine when networking?

Though it's never usually mentioned, grooming is so very important when meeting people in ANY situation, but especially in a business networking setting. Older men especially can let good grooming lapse. It's true, no matter how trite, that you never get a second chance to make a first impression.

Making sure your breath is pleasant can require constant vigilance. And I'm sure many of you have experienced someone who was not so diligent in this regard.

What are some friendly questions to ask during a one-on-one meeting with a new connection to start a conversation naturally?

General questions that have nothing to do with business can be a refreshing break from the mundane. Even the 'Are you originally from this area?' and 'Is this your first time at (venue)?' can break the ice and start a conversation about their original hometown and travels, as well as their social habits.

Tips for Crafting Memorable Networking Intros ?

Stating your name CLEARLY and your business is a great start. Relating HOW you help (customers, prospects, whoever is your target market) solve a problem, and giving the benefits of doing so can be a very effective middle part of your introduction. Always end by repeating your name and business, as many people need repetition to help them remember you to converse afterward.

The expression goes, The Fortune is in the Follow-up! What ways have you found most effective when to keep in touch with people you meet at networking events? Do you have any follow-up no no's that should be avoided?

Noting who could be a good power partner, or even better, noting who you could help with referrals, is a great way to plan your next step. The best way to follow up is usually with an in-person or virtual meeting to find common interests and ways you can benefit from each other.

PRO
Dwight Almony

COMPANY: Take Two Financial Coaching

TITLE: Owner/Lead Coach

MBX AREA CONNECTOR: York, PA

BIOGRAPHY

Throughout Dwight's adult life, he has dealt with the effects of consumer debt brought on by his father dying when he was sixteen, not learning good financial management in school, or having anyone to properly guide him financially. The lack of financial guidance contributed to both of his divorces and numerous other challenges.

In 2018, Dwight took Financial Peace University (created by Dave Ramsey). Realizing many people had never learned most of the lessons taught in Financial Peace University, Dwight became a class coordinator to help establish the class in as many churches and other places, to equip more people with these fundamentals.

After coordinating or co-coordinating several Financial Peace University classes, Dwight felt that there was something more he was to do.

In 2020, Dwight became a Financial Coach by taking the Financial Coach Master Training through Ramsey Solutions' (aka. Dave Ramsey) and launched his practice in June of that year.

Due to the COVID-19 restrictions, Dwight wasn't able to do much networking until 2021. In 2021, Dwight began networking and joined MBX in 2022. He has also participated in several other networking events and made a lot of great connections along with building relationships from them.

IF YOU'D LIKE TO CONNECT WITH DWIGHT, SCAN HIS KNO-CARD NOW.

Where is the most offbeat or weirdest place you have made a networking connection?

While driving for Uber I met a man who was starting up a local business and I invited him to an MBX luncheon.

What out of the norm ways can you suggest to new networkers to find connections?

Have genuine conversations with whomever you meet during your day so you can learn about them and how you can help them. They may not lead to a direct sale for you or be interested in joining a network group. However, they may know someone else who they would introduce you to because they have gotten to know you and know they can trust you because your focus is on helping others.

What is/are your favorite social media platforms for networking and what tips can you offer to make connections on social media?

Facebook and LinkedIn are my primary platforms for making connections. That's where most people go to look for individuals in similar or complementary fields.

What tips can you offer a new networker that will help them shine when networking?

Be genuinely interested in creating a friendship with the person and not just looking at them as a potential sale. See how you can help them acquire what they're needing.

What are some friendly questions to ask during a one-on-one meeting with a new connection to start a conversation naturally?

1. What do they do and what led them to do the work they do?

2. How long have you lived where you are? If you moved to the area, where did you live before?

3. What do you do outside of work?

Tips for Crafting Memorable Networking Intros ?

Share with them statistics about personal finances and ways that they can better manage their own finances.

The expression goes, The Fortune is in the Follow-up! What ways have you found most effective when to keep in touch with people you meet at networking events? Do you have any follow-up no no's that should be avoided?

Make sure to speak with them when I see them at another networking event or out in public. I also like to connect with them on Facebook and LinkedIn to congratulate them on milestones in their life including their birthdays.

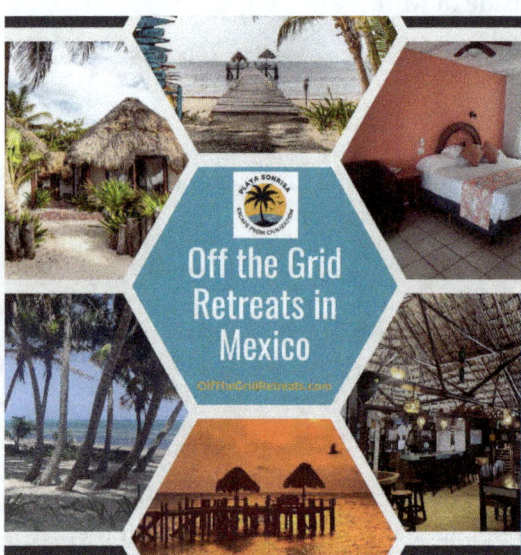

Meet the
MBX EXPERTS

SPOTLIGHT

Latara Dragoo

COMPANY: Ideal Marketing Solutions Inc.

TITLE: CEO

🎁 **FREE GIFT:** *Get your free masterclass eBook and cheat sheet -*
http://avoice.online/

BIOGRAPHY

Latara worked for Dream Homes Magazine for 18 years, climbing the career ladder, only to be laid off due to the COVID shutdown.

She decided to branch out on her own, and in April of 2020, started her own business, helping business owners and coaches pivot to the online space in the "new normal."

IF YOU'D LIKE TO CONNECT WITH LATARA, SCAN HER KNO-CARD NOW.

Where is the most offbeat or weirdest place you have made a networking connection?

A Hotel Lobby

What out of the norm ways can you suggest to new networkers to find connections?

Maintain a strong online presence through a well-designed website and strategic use of social media platforms.

Be a Resource: Share insights, resources, and connections with others without expecting an immediate return. Become a valuable resource in your network.

Seek Strategic Partnerships: Collaborate with complementary professionals, businesses, or organizations to leverage shared resources and expand your reach.

What tips can you offer a new networker that will help them shine when networking?

Listen and Give: Come with the intention of be of service to others, more than trying to get others to buy from you. Offer your advice and support generously. Be present, and listen to others.

Networking is not just about what you can gain, but also about how you can contribute and build meaningful connections. Prioritize genuine relationships, effective communication, online presence, and actively seeking opportunities for collaboration, to harness the power of networking.

What are three friendly questions to ask during a one-on-one meeting with a new connection to start a conversation naturally?

Ask things like:

1. "What initially sparked your interest in [industry/profession]?"

2. "Is there any advice or mentorship you've received throughout your career that has had a significant impact on you?"

3. "How can I be of service to you?"

The expression goes, The Fortune is in the Follow-up! What ways have you found most effective when to keep in touch with people you meet at networking events? Do you have any follow-up no no's that should be avoided?

Follow-Up and Nourish Connections: Promptly follow up after making initial connections and maintain regular interactions to nurture relationships.

Build Genuine Relationships: Focus on establishing authentic connections based on trust and mutual respect.

Anything else you'd like to share around being a Curious Connector not covered above.

Attend Networking Events with Purpose: Set clear objectives before attending networking events and focus on achieving specific goals.

Maintain a Positive Attitude: Approach networking with enthusiasm, curiosity, and a positive mindset, embracing rejection as an opportunity to learn and grow.

Andrew Friedman

COMPANY: Turning Prose Into Profits LLC

TITLE: Owner and President

BIOGRAPHY

My business is Turning Prose Into Profits LLC.

I am a writer and editor. I specialize in cover letters, resumes, and LinkedIn profiles. I also have experience writing and editing action alerts, books, brochures, corporate communications, marketing materials, newsletters, presentations, press releases, publications, reports, requests for proposals (RFPs), speeches, talking points, and content for websites.

My clients work in many different industries and professions. They include blue collar workers, as well as CEOs, CFOs, COOs, VPs, and other C-suite executives at Fortune 500 companies. I have helped high school graduates and PhDs. I have helped high school graduates and PhDs. I have also been hired by professional recruiters with decades of combined experience to write and edit cover letters, resumes, and LinkedIn profiles for their clients. A list of some of my many five-star reviews is available on my website, www.tpipllc.com.

In addition to the U.S., I have done work for clients in Australia, Austria, Brazil, Cameroon, Costa Rica, Egypt, England, the Ivory Coast, Malaysia, Switzerland, and the UAE.

I was an Associate Editor of the Law Review, and an award winning author in law school. I have written and edited legislation and regulations, including one bill that became law. My book Say Not "What If" is written as a long rhyming poem, and has glowing reviews on Amazon and Goodreads.

Please contact me for more information about my services. I can definitely improve the quality of your writing.

IF YOU'D LIKE TO CONNECT WITH ANDREW, SCAN HIS KNOCARD NOW.

Where is the most offbeat or weirdest place you have made a networking connection?

I made a networking connection in a bookstore.

What out of the norm ways can you suggest to new networkers to find connections?

1. Join networking groups and regularly attend their events.

2. Create a complete profile on LinkedIn, post at least several times a week, comment on other posts, and connect with other people in your industry.

What tips can you offer a new networker that will help them shine when networking?

1. Have a "30 second" speech that states who you are and what you do. Then ask the other person about their business.

2. Ask the other person for their business card.

3. Send the other person a LinkedIn connection request or follow-up email within 24 hours.

What are three friendly questions to ask during a one-on-one meeting with a new connection to start a conversation naturally?

1. What is your background and how did that lead you to your current position?

2. What is the biggest challenge for your business in the next year?

3. What is the most enjoyable part of your job?

The expression goes, The Fortune is in the Follow-up! What ways have you found most effective when to keep in touch with people you meet at networking events? Do you have any follow-up no no's that should be avoided?

1. Send the other person a LinkedIn connection request or follow-up email within 24 hours.

2. Set up a short Zoom meeting with the other person to discuss your businesses.

Do not try and sell your business when following-up. Doing so is presumptuous and creates the impression that you are only interested in the other person as a prospective client.

Anything else you'd like to share around being a Curious Connector not covered above.

Be yourself when networking. Relax. You need to make a good impression, but networking is not a job interview. Meeting new people and learning who they are and what they do is fun. Remembering that will help you improve your networking skills.

SPOTLIGHT

Jennifer M. Clarke

COMPANY: America's Business Coaching Academy

TITLE: CEO

BIOGRAPHY

Jen M. Clarke, America's Business Coach, has coached over 1000+ Business Owners, Entrepreneurs, Coaches, Course Creators, Agency Owners, Brand Owners, Influencers, Authors, & Professionals from all over the world. She is known for her expertise in helping Entrepreneurs and Business Owners enroll Premium, High Ticket clients within one day to a few weeks, on average! This has redeemed time and money for many of her clients, along with increasing their cash flow to be able to launch, grow and scale their businesses quickly with her QuickStart Business Method. Jen M. Clarke has many years of experience building 6 & 7 figure businesses, financial planning, not-for-profit charitable foundation work, along with many organizing events, retreats, and conferences. She has established herself as a leading authority in the field of Business Coaching.

Jen M. Clarke's ultimate gift is to help others achieve their business goals and release their treasures, gifts, & talents to the world to accelerate & maximize their potential in their life! She has helped many women and men grow their businesses, increase revenue, and achieve a significant level of success.

Jen M. Clarke specializes in helping her clients attract and enroll premium clients in almost any area of business and niche. She has developed a proven method and system, called QuickStart Business Method, that quickly provides a customized action plan for Entrepreneurs to position themselves as the authority and expert in their field and shows them how to be influential to enroll their ideal clients into their offers.

Jen M. Clarke is known for her personalized, engaging, and empowering Business Coaching, along with her Intellectual Proprietary Ideas for her clients' businesses that she creates. Jen has the ability to connect with her clients on a personal level to help create a customized Blueprint to QuickStart them on the Road to their Business Success! She uses a combination of practical steps to success, such as giving her clients the specific combination to unlock the secrets to success, building up her clients with a positive mindset, and encouraging them to overcome limitations, taking their businesses to the next level of abundance and impact for the benefit of those that her clients serve!

Jen M. Clarke is also a speaker and has delivered keynote speeches at live events, retreats, workshops, seminars, conferences and many other events both in-person and online at virtual events.

Jen M. Clarke has a commitment to excellence to helping others succeed in order to reach their full potential and have significant impact for the highest benefit of those they serve and impact in this world. Jen M. Clarke is truly America's Business Coach! (as well as an International Business Coach)

IF YOU'D LIKE TO CONNECT WITH JEN M. CLARKE, AMERICA'S BUSINESS COACH, THEN SCAN HER KNOCARD NOW.

Where is the most offbeat or weirdest place you have made a networking connection?

I had my own Radio Show called: "The Jenny Clarke Show" and the Radio Station needed to raise a lot of money in order to hire an Engineer. The local news stations thought our family had won $2.2 Million and knocked on my door while I was on a quick break at home to interview me for the daily news and I asked them to come and interview me at the Radio Station, while I was doing my Radio Show, so we could bring awareness to our need for an Engineer and the following day after the interview, an Engineer decided to contact the Radio Station to donate his services, saving the radio station at least $10,000 to $15,000!

What out of the norm ways can you suggest to new networkers to find connections?

One of the best ways that you can find networking connections is through service workers when you're going out to complete daily tasks. Connecting with grocery store employees, restaurant servers, shop owners at small markets, etc. may potentially lead to further connections through them, along with the connection with them. Many times I find myself starting conversations while I am doing daily activities in the marketplace. You would be surprised by how many individuals in the service industry have visionary ideas for business and have great connections. This is a wonderful way to network with many people on a daily basis.

What tips can you offer a new networker that will help them shine when networking?

The biggest tip I have for you is to ask your clients for testimonials for your business. Sharing the testimonials with future potential clients will help a networker shine. Clients will be more comfortable knowing that your previous clients have had a warm welcoming and inspirational experience with you and your business. The second tip I have to share is to have a bright, energetic, encouraging, and enthusiastic presence in your meetings with your clients & potential future clients. Being enthusiastic about your business will show your clients & potential future clients that your area of work is your zone of genius and that you love what you do!

What are three friendly questions to ask during a one-on-one meeting with a new connection to start a conversation naturally?

1. How can I best support you in the area that I specialize in?

2. What lights you up the most about everything that you have done, while impacting their lives for the better?

3. What interests would you like to grow & develop in your life?

The expression goes, The Fortune is in the Follow-up! What ways have you found most effective when to keep in touch with people you meet at networking events?

The most effective way to keep in touch with people that I've met at networking events is to communicate by messaging in a group or 1 to 1 Direct Messaging. Meeting those that you've networked with at least once a month, in a connection group or on a connection call, to hear about what's been new & exciting in their life and what areas they are needing support.

Anything else you'd like to share around being a Curious Connector not covered above.

The best way to network with people is to organize or to go to events that would be of interest to your ideal, potential client. Further, creating & organizing events that will attract your potential clients is one of the best ways to become a Connector.

Christine Lennips

COMPANY: It's About You

TITLE: Herb Specialist & Well-Being Expert

🎁 **FREE GIFT:** *Grab my free healthy habits check list*
https://christinelennips.com

BIOGRAPHY

Christine Lennips is a well-being expert and herbalist who has been practicing for over 35 years. She is dedicated to helping people achieve optimal health and wellness. With a passion for natural remedies and supplements, she began her journey as a practitioner after experiencing incredible results in her own health.

As she continued to expand her knowledge and skills, she developed a deep understanding of the body's interconnected systems and the underlying root causes of various health symptoms. Her unique approach combines a range of modalities alongside herbal medicine to address the whole person and create a personalized plan for each individual.

She lives in Hanover, Ontario Canada with her husband Robert. They both enjoy nature, and she loves her herbal business.

Christine's approach and extensive experience have helped countless individuals overcome a wide range of health concerns. Her commitment to ongoing education, and her dedication to her clients' well-being has made her a trusted and valued member of the holistic health community.

Whether you're struggling with a chronic health condition or simply looking to optimize your overall wellness, she can help you achieve your goals and live your best life!

IF YOU'D LIKE TO CONNECT WITH CHRISTINE, SCAN HER KNO-CARD NOW.

Where is the most offbeat or weirdest place you have made a networking connection?

In the line waiting for the ladies restroom

What out of the norm ways can you suggest to new networkers to find connections?

Depending on your business, look at local in-person trade shows. They get overlooked by many businesses and are a great way to meet the people of your town or city and the surrounding area.

What tips can you offer a new networker that will help them shine when networking?

Join the Chamber of Commerce. Attend their events and network with the local businesses. You never know what joint ventures and collaborations you may be able to create!

On-line or In-person, ask questions of them to learn what people they are looking for to help them in their business. It is a great way to get to them and be of help to them. It often comes back to you in more ways than you would expect!!!

What are some friendly questions to ask during a one-on-one meeting with a new connection to start a conversation naturally?

Since I have been in business for 36 years now, I love to know - How long have you been working where you are positioned? What attracted you to the industry you are in?

The expression goes, The Fortune is in the Follow-up! What ways have you found most effective when to keep in touch with people you meet at networking events? Do you have any follow-up no no's that should be avoided?

Make it your responsibility to follow up with the other party! Taking a card or putting their name and number in your phone, writing down their email address does no good if you don't actually reach out. Interested people can easily get busy. They may have misplaced your information. If you don't reach out, the answer is no!

Anything else you'd like to share around being a Curious Connector not covered above.

Feel comfortable to ask curiosity questions to learn more about what they do and where their passions lie. People getting to know each other and building rapport and trust can build strong relationships!

Laureen Shefchik

COMPANY: HeartFlow Energy

TITLE: Founder

BIOGRAPHY

Hello, I'm Laureen Shefchik, Energy Coder and Intuitive Coach. Imagine if you were living paycheck to paycheck, feeling stuck, or in physical pain. Imagine if you felt alone in a houseful of people, if you have lost friendships, family members, or fulfillment. The work I do through energy coding releases blocked negative energy that keeps you stuck and eventually manifests as physical pain. I have worked with hundreds of clients that have broken through negative energy barriers to create the life they love! I love serving people in this unconditional way, and giving them their lives back!

IF YOU'D LIKE TO CONNECT WITH LAUREEN, SCAN HER KNO-CARD NOW.

Where is the most offbeat or weirdest place you have made a networking connection?

Waiting for a Spa treatment in Phoenix, AZ! There were three of us waiting for our next spa treatments, and started talking. One of them was a "connector type" and connected me to her best friend, right there! She was celebrating her 60th birthday and needed my services for letting go of past baggage that was keeping her stuck!

What out of the norm ways can you suggest to new networkers to find connections?

Get involved in groups that meet in person or online, volunteer in your community, state or national groups specific to things you all have in common. Meeting people and forming friendships and then doing business to connect through the friendship is a much stronger bond than the old ways of networking!

What tips can you offer a new networker that will help them shine when networking?

Get really clear on who you are serving and lead with love for the person you are serving! It's not about you and your bottom line. Whatever your product, service is you provide, get clear on how it will better their life, their home, their business. When you get really clear on how you can serve them the best way possible it will all fall into place because it is not about you, ever.

What are three friendly questions to ask during a one-on-one meeting with a new connection to start a conversation naturally?

1. What is important to you, at home, at work, in relationships?

2. I'm curious about what you do, can you tell me more?

3. What is one thing you would change if you could?

The expression goes, The Fortune is in the Follow-up! What ways have you found most effective when to keep in touch with people you meet at networking events? Do you have any follow-up no no's that should be avoided?

If I have made a connection with you and we had a real conversation and both said we would be interested in reconnecting outside of this event, then green light to follow up. Real connections and building friendships as a bridge to business building is a strong foundation.

Do not spam everyone after an event, that is so not a thing anymore, so just do not do it!

Anything else you'd like to share around being a Curious Connector not covered above.

Connections are as necessary as the air we breathe. We all need human connection. The year 2020 wreaked havoc on human connection. Many of the clients I deal with are still releasing betrayal, and unworthiness from the trauma of 2020. Find your people, find new friendships through what you naturally are attracted to. Look at who you are, your standards, your convictions, your values and find people who are like minded. We are the same so much more than we are different. Embrace humanity as a whole energy field and be vulnerable!

Israel Carberry

COMPANY: Green Hollow Technology LLC

TITLE: Lead Consultant

BIOGRAPHY

Down a quarter mile dirt driveway off a lonely highway cutting between two sandstone bluffs on the windswept Great Plains of Wyoming, where party lines and shortwave radio are still the normal means of communication in 1988, a young boy sits hunched over a spiral bound reference book to the GW-BASIC programming syntax, desperately seeking deeper magic for making the Tandy 1000EX before him obey his every whim.

Since that fateful time of his early life, Israel Carberry has been enthralled with finding better ways of wizarding what we will from these strange creatures we have crafted from earthen materials, animated with lightening, and named "computer". He has been employed by a variety of companies over the decades to engineer software, and has progressed through a series of technical lead and management roles. Building on his experience, he has established his own venture, consulting companies and organizations to help them improve their teams, systems, and business functions related to delivering software.

Israel lives with his wife of 23 years in a small Texas town, where he still isn't used to the heat and humidity. He has two grown sons who are much cooler than him, and a bewildering number of stray cats who won't go away.

IF YOU'D LIKE TO CONNECT WITH ISRAEL, SCAN HIS KNO-CARD NOW.

Where is the most offbeat or weirdest place you have made a networking connection?

I alerted a homeless guy to a car turning left into the intersection we were both crossing, and we started talking as we walked. He gave me the absolutely best startup pitch I have ever heard. It was for an app connecting people going through rehab to every other service they might need. I gave him my business card.

What out of the norm ways can you suggest to new networkers to find connections?

Make eye contact and smile with people EVERYWHERE. Just make it a habit.

What tips can you offer a new networker that will help them shine when networking?

If you feel anxiety when meeting and talking with strangers, whether in person or on a video call, you can trick your brain into "recognizing" someone as a friend. Look at someone, and create a fake flash of memory as if you had spent a relaxing evening at a dinner party having great conversation with them. Don't try to imagine what happened, just see their face in a snapshot moment with that feeling of familiarity. Then talk with them and create real memories!

What are three friendly questions to ask during a one-on-one meeting with a new connection to start a conversation naturally?

I have found that I connect best with people who are always learning and curious, so I want to know what they've been learning recently. What's your go-to for learning - books, podcasts, or something else? What book / podcast / etc. has made the most impact on you? What have you been reading / listening to recently?

The expression goes, The Fortune is in the Follow-up! What ways have you found most effective when to keep in touch with people you meet at networking events? Do you have any follow-up no no's that should be avoided?

I create an event on my calendar to follow up with a person immediately after talking with them, or I'll forget. I can always move the event later, so I put it for the soonest time I know I'll be at my computer. When following up, the last thing I want to do is talk about myself, which is a major turn-off when people do that to me, so I look for something about them or what they do that I'm honestly curious and want to ask them about.

Anything else you'd like to share around being a Curious Connector not covered above.

Read *Give and Take* by Adam Grant. Learn to recognize the Givers, and prioritize those relationships. And, of course, be a Giver yourself.

Jacki Channer

COMPANY: Almaize

TITLE: CEO

BIOGRAPHY

I have been helping my clients for over 40 years not to be afraid of Money 😊😊 I love helping people understand how money works. I like to know the rules of money, once you know the rules—you get the money. We take the mystery out of money and show people how to use it for the tool that it really is. We are not married to loans; that's what we try to teach.

At Almaize, we do several types of financing. We do business financing to help businesses get up and running. We do unsecured financing which helps both investors and businesses get up and running. We do commercial and construction financing. We have seed money to get you the fix and flip money. We show you how to rehab a property. Once you have rehabbed the property, we show you how to sell it immediately or rent it out, with property management if needed. I specialize in investors and showing them how to build that RE portfolio they can retire on and not just a 401k. We show investors how to get in the game.

IF YOU'D LIKE TO CONNECT WITH JACKI, SCAN HER KNOCARD NOW.

Where is the most offbeat or weirdest place you have made a networking connection?

At a Funeral and Hospital

What out of the norm ways can you suggest to new networkers to find connections?

Go to educational seminars where you will find the type of clientele you wish to network with.

What tips can you offer a new networker that will help them shine when networking?

Be yourself and be genuine. People can feel that as soon as you speak to them and look them right in the eye.

What are three friendly questions to ask during a one-on-one meeting with a new connection to start a conversation naturally?

Where was the weirdest place you picked up business?

Who is your favorite client to date?

What was the funniest thing that happened to you on a sales call or while you were conducting business that really made you laugh?

The expression goes, The Fortune is in the Follow-up! What ways have you found most effective when to keep in touch with people you meet at networking events? Do you have any follow-up no no's that should be avoided?

Just the old fashioned way sending birthday greetings and anniversary greetings ..they are very effective.

Blaney Teal
Founder of MBX

SPOTLIGHT

Ronald McElhose

COMPANY: M&P Business Funding

TITLE: Business Funding Representative

BIOGRAPHY

Mack has been Vice President of 2 Companies and recently retired to concentrate on helping businesses with their financial needs. Loans for any need from $10,000 to $1,000,000! Just contact Mack today and we can get the ball rolling quickly!

IF YOU'D LIKE TO CONNECT WITH RONALD, SCAN HIS KNO-CARD NOW.

Where is the most offbeat or weirdest place you have made a networking connection?

On a carnival Cruise ship! Went on vacation and connected with two business owners!

What out of the norm ways can you suggest to new networkers to find connections?

I always suggest everyone to join MBX. One of the best ways to connect to other businesses.

What tips can you offer a new networker that will help them shine when networking?

Always suggest ways for the business to improve! You can offer your services during your conversation so you are not pushy and more inviting!

What are three friendly questions to ask during a one-on-one meeting with a new connection to start a conversation naturally?

What do you like about your job? Anything you don't like? What do you like to do during your free time?

The expression goes, The Fortune is in the Follow-up! What ways have you found most effective when to keep in touch with people you meet at networking events? Do you have any follow-up no no's that should be avoided?

I always like to connect with folks by email or Text messages.

Anything else you'd like to share around being a Curious Connector not covered above.

Always share your success stories! They will allow others to see what they might accomplish in their own business!

Meet the

MBX EXPERTS

QUOTES BY OTHER BUSINESSES WE RECOMMEND

Diana Ringer

COMPANY: More Expert

BIOGRAPHY

Diana has a degree in Business Information Systems and has over 20 years of experience in programming/web development and systems design & implementation. She has a passion for teaching and training in business & personal development principles. Published author.

IF YOU'D LIKE TO CONNECT WITH DIANA, SCAN HER KNOCARD NOW.

FAVORITE QUOTE

"Networking is like dating. It's about building long-term strategic relationships with people who ARE or KNOW your perfect niche client. People move from strangers to clients in 5 discrete phases. Each phase has its own objectives and methods. Don't rush. Without clients, you aren't in business."

Genevieve Quenum

COMPANY: Growth Catalyst Service LLC

TITLE: Founder and manager

EMAIL: growthcatalystservice@gmail.com

BIOGRAPHY

I'm a Maxwell Leadership-Certified Coach-Trainer-Speaker and a professional Christian Life and Mental Health Coach. My passion is setting people up for success and unlocking potential through personal growth and leadership development from a Christian perspective. My Coaching is empowered by The Maxwell D.I.S.C Method because when you know yourself you can grow yourself.

IF YOU'D LIKE TO CONNECT WITH GENEVIEVE, SCAN HER KNOCARD NOW.

FAVORITE QUOTE

"You don't overcome challenges by making them smaller but by making yourself bigger."

JOHN C. MAXWELL

Lucie Rosa-Stagi

COMPANY: Launch Lab Academy

TITLE: Community Builder

BIOGRAPHY

Launch Lab Academy: Inspiring Coaches Worldwide Meet Mike, Lucie, Athena, and Eden - visionary expat mentors breaking boundaries and speaking to new coaches across 6 continents. With expertise in personal branding, AI-powered marketing, and sales, they're the go-to mentors for diverse backgrounds. Since 2018, they've united to form Launch Lab Academy, boasting 60 years of combined experience and helping 1000+ coaches realize their dreams. Partnering with industry giants like Tony Robbins & Dean Graziosi, they lead the charge in digital knowledge. Launch Lab Academy stands out for its commitment to helping older generations embrace the digital era. Their dedication earned them the 2024 Global Recognition Award, inspiring generations to pursue entrepreneurial dreams, regardless of age. Join us in shaping legacies and empowering coaches worldwide.

IF YOU'D LIKE TO CONNECT WITH LUCIE, SCAN HER KNOCARD NOW.

FAVORITE QUOTE

"Your greatest asset is your mindset."

Sonia Pace

COMPANY: Sydney Sheppard Books

TITLE: CEO

BIOGRAPHY

I create and publish books designed for Parents, Teens & Young Adults to unlock their full potential, starting with their mindset.

IF YOU'D LIKE TO CONNECT WITH SONIA, SCAN HER KNO-CARD NOW.

FAVORITE QUOTE

"Luck doesn't just happen, you create it by sparking up a conversation with a total stranger."

Steven Hessler

COMPANY: Land Flipping Secrets

TITLE: Owner

BIOGRAPHY

Steven Hessler is a true "Rags to Riches" story. He went from flat broke and penniless in Scotland to buying a beachfront resort in Mexico just 18 months later. This transformation was possible thanks to his unconventional land flipping techniques that go beyond what typical "gurus" teach. He even offers a 100% Student Guarantee you will get your investment back with your first deal!

READY TO LEARN A SIDE HUSTLE OR A NEW CAREER, REACH OUT TO STEVEN THROUGH HIS KNOCARD.

FAVORITE QUOTE

"Networking isn't how many people you know; it's how many people know you."

TammyStar Workman-Lopez

COMPANY: Sparks Hope ~ Anxiety Relief, Relationships, & Mindset Reset Coaching

TITLE: Hypnocoach & Mindset Reset Coach | Entrepreneurs & Couples

BIOGRAPHY

I am Tammy Workman-Lopez Anxiety Relief, Relationship, & Mindset Reset HypnoCoach.

My work equips entrepreneurial individuals and couples to find relief from communication blocks, perfectionism, and negative thinking while creating action-taking step-by-step results to prosper in their lives and businesses.

IF YOU'D LIKE TO CONNECT WITH TAMMY, SCAN HER KNOCARD NOW.

FAVORITE QUOTE

"Networking is more than just sharing what you do; it's about revealing who you are. With over a decade of networking and speaking experience and having reached thousands of women entrepreneurs, I've seen the power of sharing your story and the passion that drives you. As a Hypnocoach & Mindset Reset Coach in Orlando, Florida, I host the Powerful Women's Networking event every 2nd Friday of the month. When you authentically connect with others and let your light shine, they're not just buying from you; they're connecting with the beautiful energy of who you are. Join us at our next event and experience the magic of genuine connections."